UNDERSTANDING DEPRESSION

Comprehensive Guide To Symptoms, Causes, Diagnosis, And Effective Treatments For Mental Health And Wellness

DR. LINCOLN WAYLON

DISCLAIMER

This book contains information that should only be used for educational and informational reasons; it is not meant to be used as a source of medical or psychological advice. The author's studies, life experiences, and expertise in the area of health and wellness served as the foundation for the content. It should not, however, be used in place of expert counsel, a diagnosis, or medical care.

Any queries you may have about a physical or mental health issue should always be directed toward the advice of a licensed healthcare provider or mental health specialist. With regard to the efficacy or outcomes of the methods or suggestions included in this book, the author and publisher make no representations or warranties.

Any information or methods in this book are used entirely at the reader's own risk and discretion. The material provided here may be used or misused, and neither the author nor the publisher will be held responsible for any results, losses, or negative impacts.

Keep in mind that everyone has different demands and reactions to health and wellness routines. Any health and wellness plans you implement must be customized to your particular circumstances, and you should speak with experts to make sure the plans meet your needs.

TABLE OF CONTENTS

ABOUT THE BOOK

Understanding Depression is a vital resource that delves deeply into one of the most pervasive mental health challenges of our time. This book serves as an essential guide for both individuals struggling with depression and those supporting them. It begins with an overview of depression, clarifying the difference between ordinary sadness and clinical depression. Emphasizing the importance of early detection, it introduces self-assessment tools and underscores the necessity of seeking timely help and intervention.

The book then explores how depression uniquely affects children and adolescents. It provides insights into symptoms specific to younger populations and how depression manifests differently in children. Factors contributing to youth depression are discussed, along with strategies for parents and guardians to effectively support their children. The text also covers professional treatment options available for young people, ensuring a comprehensive understanding of the support systems in place for this vulnerable group.

Adult experiences with depression are addressed with sensitivity to the unique symptoms and challenges faced. The book examines how depression impacts work and family life, identifies common triggers and risk factors, and presents effective coping strategies. It also offers a thorough exploration of treatment approaches and resources tailored to adults, equipping readers with the knowledge to navigate their journey with depression.

A significant portion of the book is dedicated to understanding depression in the context of co-occurring disorders. It highlights the prevalence of mental health disorders that commonly accompany depression, such as anxiety and substance abuse. The interactions between these conditions are explored, alongside integrated treatment approaches designed to address dual diagnoses. Support strategies for managing co-occurring conditions are also included, providing a holistic view of comprehensive mental health care.

Treatment options for depression are thoroughly reviewed, covering various psychotherapies like Cognitive Behavioral Therapy (CBT) and Dialectical Behavior Therapy (DBT). The book explains medication options, how they work, and the role of complementary and alternative treatments. Lifestyle changes that can aid in managing depression are discussed, and guidance is provided on creating a personalized treatment plan to meet individual needs.

Self-help and coping strategies are also a key focus. The book guides readers in developing healthy routines and habits, managing stress, and the importance of social support.

Techniques for mindfulness and relaxation are outlined, along with strategies for building resilience and practicing self-care, all crucial for navigating the ups and downs of depression.

Navigating professional help is another critical aspect covered in detail. Readers learn about different types of mental health professionals and how to find the right therapist or counselor. The book sets expectations for therapy sessions, provides tips for working effectively with healthcare providers, and offers advice on advocacy and navigating insurance, ensuring that readers can make informed decisions about their mental health care.

The impact of depression on relationships is addressed, focusing on how it affects interactions with family and friends. Strategies for communicating with loved ones about depression are provided, alongside tips for maintaining healthy relationships and supporting partners and caregivers. The role of support groups and community resources is highlighted, emphasizing the importance of a strong support network.

The book offers practical advice for preventing relapse and maintaining recovery. It includes guidance on recognizing early warning signs of relapse, developing strategies for long-term management, and the importance of ongoing support. Readers are encouraged to build a relapse prevention plan and set and achieve personal goals, fostering a sense of empowerment and control over their mental health journey.

The detailed FAQs section addresses common concerns, such as distinguishing depression from a temporary bad mood, dealing with suicidal thoughts, finding affordable mental health care, and asking the right questions when discussing treatment options with a doctor. This comprehensive guide aims to elevate understanding, support well-being, and provide practical tools for managing depression effectively.

CHAPTER ONE

OVERVIEW OF DEPRESSION

IDENTIFYING SIGNS AND SYMPTOMS

Recognizing the signs and symptoms of depression is crucial for timely intervention. Common indicators include persistent feelings of sadness, hopelessness, or emptiness that last for weeks or months. Individuals may also experience significant changes in appetite or sleep patterns, either eating or sleeping too much or too little.

Loss of interest or pleasure in activities once enjoyed, coupled with fatigue or low energy, is also prevalent symptoms. Cognitive impairments, such as difficulty concentrating or making decisions, further characterize depressive episodes, impacting daily functioning.

Physical symptoms can manifest alongside emotional ones, including unexplained aches or pains, headaches, or digestive problems.

Changes in personal hygiene or neglect of responsibilities might signal the presence of depression. Emotional instability, such as excessive irritability or mood swings, can also be indicative. It is essential to observe whether these symptoms are pervasive and persistent rather than transient, as chronic patterns are more indicative of clinical depression.

Addressing these symptoms early can prevent worsening conditions. Individuals noticing these signs in themselves or others should consider them as serious and potentially debilitating. Accurate identification involves reflecting on the duration, intensity, and impact of these symptoms on daily life, which can provide critical insights into whether professional help might be needed.

DIFFERENTIATING BETWEEN NORMAL SADNESS AND CLINICAL DEPRESSION

Normal sadness, which everyone experiences from time to time, is usually a response to specific life events, such as a personal loss or disappointment. This type of sadness generally fades as time passes or as the situation improves. Clinical depression, however, is more profound and persistent. It is characterized by a prolonged duration of symptoms, lasting for at least two weeks or more, and significantly interferes with an individual's ability to function daily.

The intensity of clinical depression often exceeds that of normal sadness. While sadness might be a natural emotional response, clinical depression includes a range of symptoms that deeply affect a person's emotional state and physical health. This includes a pervasive sense of worthlessness or excessive guilt and a drastic reduction in productivity and motivation. Additionally, clinical depression may involve more severe symptoms like suicidal thoughts or self-harm, which are not typical of normal sadness.

Understanding the difference is key for proper management and treatment. Normal sadness generally resolves with time and supportive interventions, while clinical depression requires a comprehensive approach involving medical and psychological support. If symptoms align more with the latter, it is crucial to seek professional evaluation to differentiate and address them effectively.

THE ROLE OF SELF-ASSESSMENT TOOLS

Self-assessment tools are valuable resources for individuals to gauge their mental health status and identify symptoms of depression. These tools often consist of questionnaires or checklists that evaluate emotional and behavioral patterns, helping individuals reflect on their mental well-being. For instance, tools like the Patient Health Questionnaire (PHQ-9) or the Beck Depression Inventory are designed to assess the severity of depressive symptoms and provide insights into the need for professional evaluation.

Using self-assessment tools involves completing the questionnaires honestly, and reflecting on current feelings, behaviors, and overall mood.

The results can offer a preliminary understanding of one's mental health and indicate whether symptoms align with clinical depression. These tools help in recognizing the need for further professional assessment and treatment, serving as an initial step in the diagnostic process.

Although self-assessment tools are useful, they are not substitutes for professional diagnosis. They should be used as part of a broader evaluation process that includes consultations with mental health professionals. Accurate diagnosis and effective treatment planning depend on comprehensive assessments conducted by healthcare providers, making self-assessment a complementary but not sole method for understanding one's mental health.

IMPORTANCE OF EARLY DETECTION

Early detection of depression is vital for effective management and recovery. Recognizing symptoms early allows individuals to seek help before the condition worsens.

This proactive approach can prevent the escalation of symptoms, reducing the risk of severe emotional and physical complications. Early intervention often leads to more effective treatment outcomes, as addressing the condition in its initial stages can make therapies more impactful and prevent long-term impairment.

Timely detection involves paying attention to subtle changes in mood, behavior, and functioning. Individuals and their support networks should be vigilant for early signs of depression and consider professional help if symptoms persist beyond a typical duration of sadness. Early intervention not only improves the chances of recovery but also helps in preventing relapses and ensuring ongoing mental well-being.

The importance of early detection cannot be overstated, as it significantly influences the effectiveness of treatment and the quality of life. Encouraging regular mental health check-ups and fostering open conversations about emotional well-being can aid in identifying depression early and ensuring that appropriate support is provided promptly.

SEEKING HELP AND INTERVENTION

Seeking help and intervention for depression is crucial for effective treatment and management. If symptoms of depression are persistent or severe, reaching out to mental health professionals such as psychologists, psychiatrists, or counselors is essential. These professionals can provide accurate diagnoses, therapeutic interventions, and medication if necessary, tailored to the individual's specific needs.

Engaging in therapy, such as cognitive-behavioral therapy (CBT) or other counseling methods, can help individuals understand and manage their symptoms. Support groups and peer support can also be beneficial, offering a sense of community and shared experiences. Medication may be prescribed for managing chemical imbalances that contribute to depression, and it is essential to follow treatment plans as directed by healthcare providers.

Encouraging open discussions about mental health and reducing the stigma associated with seeking help can facilitate earlier intervention. Individuals should be proactive about their mental health, seeking support when needed and following through with treatment plans to improve their quality of life and overall well-being.

CHAPTER TWO

UNDERSTANDING DEPRESSION IN CHILDREN AND ADOLESCENTS

SYMPTOMS SPECIFIC TO YOUNGER POPULATIONS

Depression in children and adolescents can manifest differently compared to adults, with symptoms often reflecting their developmental stage. Younger children may show increased irritability, frequent temper tantrums, and withdrawal from previously enjoyed activities. They might express feelings of sadness through physical complaints like stomachaches or headaches rather than directly talking about their emotions. Observing changes in behavior, such as difficulty concentrating or a sudden drop in academic performance, can also be indicative of depression in younger populations.

Adolescents, on the other hand, may display more nuanced signs of depression. They might become more withdrawn, engage in risky behaviors, or show a significant shift in their social circles.

Mood swings, feelings of hopelessness, and changes in sleep patterns are common. Adolescents may also exhibit changes in their appetite or weight, and a loss of interest in activities they once enjoyed, which can be a subtle but clear signal of underlying depressive issues.

Understanding these symptoms requires attentive observation from parents, teachers, and caregivers. Recognizing the behavioral and emotional changes specific to younger individuals can help in early identification and intervention. It's crucial to differentiate between typical developmental mood swings and potential signs of depression to ensure appropriate support and treatment are provided.

HOW DEPRESSION MANIFESTS IN CHILDREN

Depression in children can manifest through a range of behavioral and emotional changes. Younger children may exhibit a marked decline in their interest in play, a common indicator of emotional distress.

They may also demonstrate a lack of enthusiasm for social interactions, which can be particularly evident in settings like school or during family activities. These children might also have trouble sleeping, either experiencing insomnia or oversleeping, along with changes in their eating habits.

In contrast, adolescents often show more complex manifestations of depression. They might struggle with feelings of worthlessness or inadequacy, which can affect their self-esteem and social interactions. Additionally, moodiness or anger that seems out of proportion to the situation can be a sign of underlying depression.

Adolescents may also engage in self-destructive behaviors or substance abuse as a way to cope with their emotional pain.

Recognizing these manifestations involves understanding the typical behaviors and emotional responses of children at various developmental stages.

Parents and caregivers should be vigilant for signs that go beyond normal mood fluctuations and seek professional help if depressive symptoms persist or worsen over time.

FACTORS CONTRIBUTING TO YOUTH DEPRESSION

Several factors contribute to the development of depression in children and adolescents, including genetic, environmental, and psychological influences. A family history of depression can increase the risk of similar issues in younger individuals, suggesting a genetic predisposition.

Environmental factors such as exposure to trauma, abuse, or neglect can significantly impact a child's mental health and contribute to the onset of depressive symptoms.

Peer relationships and social pressures also play a crucial role in youth depression. Bullying, social exclusion, and the pressure to conform can create significant stress, leading to feelings of inadequacy and depression. Additionally, academic stress and family conflicts are significant contributors, as children may feel overwhelmed or unsupported during challenging times.

Understanding these contributing factors involves examining both individual and environmental elements that influence mental health. Addressing these factors requires a holistic approach, including family support, school interventions, and strategies to mitigate environmental stressors to help manage and prevent depression in young people.

STRATEGIES FOR PARENTS AND GUARDIANS

Parents and guardians can play a pivotal role in addressing and managing depression in children and adolescents. Open communication is essential; creating an environment where children feel safe to express their feelings without judgment can significantly impact their emotional well-being. It's important for parents to actively listen and validate their child's experiences, helping them feel understood and supported.

Establishing consistent routine and encouraging healthy lifestyle choices, such as regular physical activity and balanced nutrition, can also help manage symptoms of depression.

Engaging in family activities and promoting positive social interactions can provide emotional support and strengthen family bonds. Parents should also be attentive to changes in their child's behavior and seek professional help if they notice persistent or worsening symptoms.

Implementing strategies that foster a supportive and empathetic home environment can be crucial for a child's recovery. Encouraging open dialogue, maintaining a structured routine, and seeking professional guidance when necessary can significantly contribute to managing and alleviating depressive symptoms in young people.

PROFESSIONAL TREATMENT OPTIONS FOR YOUNG PEOPLE

Professional treatment options for young people with depression often involve a combination of psychotherapy, medication, and family support. Cognitive Behavioral Therapy (CBT) is a commonly used therapeutic approach that helps children and adolescents identify and modify negative thought patterns and behaviors. It provides practical strategies for managing stress and coping with depressive symptoms.

In some cases, medication may be prescribed to help balance neurotransmitters in the brain, particularly if the depression is severe or does not improve with therapy alone. Antidepressants like selective serotonin reuptake inhibitors (SSRIs) are often used, but their use requires careful monitoring by a healthcare professional due to potential side effects.

Collaborating with mental health professionals, including psychologists, psychiatrists, and counselors, ensures that young people receive comprehensive care tailored to their specific needs. Family involvement in treatment can enhance effectiveness, as it helps address underlying issues and provides a supportive environment for the young person's recovery.

CHAPTER THREE

DEPRESSION IN ADULTS

ADULT-SPECIFIC SYMPTOMS AND CHALLENGES

Depression in adults often manifests through a range of symptoms that can disrupt daily functioning and overall well-being. Common symptoms include persistent feelings of sadness, hopelessness, and a lack of interest in previously enjoyable activities. Adults may also experience significant changes in appetite and sleep patterns, including insomnia or excessive sleeping. Cognitive difficulties such as trouble concentrating, making decisions, or remembering things are also prevalent, impacting their ability to perform daily tasks effectively.

The challenges faced by adults with depression are compounded by their responsibilities and life circumstances. Work performance may suffer due to reduced productivity, absenteeism, or difficulty engaging in work-related tasks.

Relationships with family and friends can become strained as the individual may withdraw socially or struggle with communicating their feelings, leading to misunderstandings and conflict. The combined pressure of personal and professional obligations can exacerbate feelings of inadequacy and frustration.

Additionally, adults might encounter specific challenges such as the stigma associated with mental health issues, which can deter them from seeking help. They may also face difficulties balancing treatment with their responsibilities, including managing time for therapy or medication amidst busy schedules. Understanding these symptoms and challenges is crucial for addressing depression effectively and ensuring appropriate support is provided.

Depression can have a profound impact on an individual's work life, leading to decreased productivity and job performance.

Adults may find it challenging to maintain focus, meet deadlines, or engage effectively in team activities. The emotional toll of depression can result in frequent absences from work or even job loss, which adds additional stress and financial strain. Employers and colleagues may also struggle to understand the underlying issues, leading to potential misunderstandings or lack of support in the workplace.

Family life can also be significantly affected by an adult's depression. The emotional and behavioral changes associated with depression can create tension and conflict within family dynamics. Family members may feel helpless, frustrated, or confused about how to support their loved one, which can strain relationships. Responsibilities within the household may become overwhelming for the depressed individual, leading to neglect of household duties and further contributing to familial stress.

The impact on work and family life underscores the importance of addressing depression proactively. Open communication with employers and family members, seeking appropriate support, and implementing strategies to manage symptoms can help mitigate these effects.

By recognizing and addressing the challenges depression presents in these areas, individuals and their support networks can work towards improving overall well-being and functionality.

COMMON TRIGGERS AND RISK FACTORS

Several factors can trigger or exacerbate depression in adults, including both internal and external influences. Stressful life events such as financial problems, relationship issues, or significant life changes can act as catalysts for depression.

Additionally, unresolved trauma or past experiences can contribute to the onset or worsening of depressive symptoms. Identifying these triggers is essential for managing and preventing further episodes of depression.

Risk factors for depression include genetic predisposition, with a family history of mental health issues increasing susceptibility. Biological factors, such as imbalances in brain chemicals or hormonal changes, can also play a role in the development of depression. Lifestyle factors, including poor diet, lack of exercise, and substance abuse, further compound the risk. Recognizing these risk factors allows individuals and healthcare providers to address underlying issues and implement preventative measures.

Understanding common triggers and risk factors provides valuable insight into the development and management of depression. By identifying and addressing these factors, individuals can better manage their mental health and reduce the likelihood of experiencing severe depressive episodes. Early intervention and tailored support strategies can help mitigate the impact of these triggers and improve overall mental health.

EFFECTIVE COPING STRATEGIES

Coping with depression involves a combination of strategies designed to manage symptoms and improve overall well-being. Regular physical activity is a key coping strategy, as exercise has been shown to boost mood and reduce symptoms of depression. Engaging in activities such as walking, yoga, or strength training can improve both physical and mental health. Establishing a consistent exercise routine can provide a valuable outlet for stress and enhance mood.

Developing a supportive social network is another effective strategy for managing depression. Connecting with friends, family, or support groups can provide emotional support and reduce feelings of isolation.

Sharing experiences and receiving encouragement from others who understand can be immensely beneficial. Additionally, practicing mindfulness and relaxation techniques, such as meditation or deep breathing exercises, can help manage stress and improve emotional resilience.

Implementing healthy lifestyle habits, including maintaining a balanced diet, getting adequate sleep, and setting realistic goals, contributes to effective coping. Establishing a daily routine and setting small, achievable goals can help create a sense of structure and purpose.

By incorporating these coping strategies into daily life, individuals can better manage their depression and work towards improving their overall quality of life.

TREATMENT APPROACHES AND RESOURCES

Effective treatment for depression typically involves a combination of therapy, medication, and lifestyle changes. Psychotherapy, including cognitive-behavioral therapy (CBT) and interpersonal therapy (IPT), is commonly used to address negative thought patterns and improve coping skills.

These therapies provide valuable tools for managing depression and offer a structured approach to understanding and overcoming symptoms.

Medication may also be prescribed to help manage depression. Antidepressants, such as selective serotonin reuptake inhibitors (SSRIs) or serotonin-norepinephrine reuptake inhibitors (SNRIs), can help balance brain chemicals and alleviate symptoms. Individuals need to work closely with their healthcare provider to find the right medication and dosage for their specific needs, and to monitor any potential side effects.

In addition to therapy and medication, various resources are available to support individuals with depression. Support groups, both in-person and online, offer a platform for sharing experiences and receiving support from others with similar challenges.

CHAPTER FOUR

DEPRESSION AND CO-OCCURRING DISORDERS

COMMON MENTAL HEALTH DISORDERS ASSOCIATED WITH DEPRESSION

Depression frequently coexists with various other mental health disorders, each compounding the complexity of diagnosis and treatment. Anxiety disorders are among the most common comorbid conditions, where persistent worry and fear exacerbate feelings of sadness and hopelessness. Individuals with depression often experience panic attacks or generalized anxiety, which can intensify their depressive symptoms, making it essential to address both conditions simultaneously for effective management.

Another prevalent co-occurring disorder is substance abuse. People may use alcohol or drugs as a coping mechanism for their depression, which can create a cycle of dependency and worsen mental health issues. This self-medication can lead to increased severity of both depression and substance use, necessitating integrated treatment strategies to address both the addiction and the underlying depressive disorder.

Personality disorders, such as borderline personality disorder, are also commonly seen alongside depression. The instability in mood, self-image, and interpersonal relationships typical of these disorders can significantly aggravate depressive symptoms. A comprehensive treatment approach must consider these overlapping symptoms and address the complexities of managing multiple disorders simultaneously.

Depression and anxiety often interact in a manner that magnifies the distress experienced by individuals. When someone suffers from both conditions, the constant state of nervousness and apprehension associated with anxiety can deepen feelings of sadness and hopelessness characteristic of depression. The cycle of worry can prevent individuals from seeking help or engaging in treatment, making it crucial to address both disorders in a unified treatment plan.

Substance abuse, particularly alcohol and drug use, is frequently a response to the overwhelming feelings of depression. Individuals might misuse substances to numb emotional pain or escape from their depressive state.

This misuse can create a vicious cycle, where substance abuse worsens depressive symptoms and complicates the treatment process. Integrated treatment that targets both depression and substance abuse is essential to breaking this cycle and achieving recovery.

Additionally, depression's impact on cognitive functions, such as decision-making and impulse control, often exacerbates problems with substance use.

People struggling with depression may find it harder to make rational decisions, leading to an increased likelihood of engaging in risky behaviors or substance misuse. Addressing these issues concurrently through a comprehensive approach can improve outcomes and support long-term recovery.

INTEGRATED TREATMENT APPROACHES

Integrated treatment approaches are crucial for managing co-occurring disorders effectively. This involves a coordinated effort between mental health professionals to address both depression and its associated conditions, such as anxiety or substance abuse.

Treatments may include a combination of psychotherapy, medication, and lifestyle changes tailored to address the complexities of each condition simultaneously.

For instance, cognitive-behavioral therapy (CBT) is a common method used to treat both depression and anxiety. CBT helps individuals identify and challenge negative thought patterns, which can alleviate symptoms of both disorders. Additionally, pharmacotherapy, such as antidepressants and anxiolytics, may be prescribed to manage the biochemical imbalances contributing to these conditions.

Integrated treatment also involves the use of support systems, including support groups and community resources, to provide a holistic approach to recovery. This approach ensures that all aspects of an individual's mental health are addressed, promoting overall well-being and reducing the risk of relapse.

RECOGNIZING DUAL DIAGNOSIS

Recognizing a dual diagnosis is essential for effective treatment planning. Dual diagnosis refers to the presence of both a primary mental health disorder, such as depression and a co-occurring disorder, such as substance abuse or anxiety. Accurate diagnosis requires a thorough evaluation by mental health professionals who can distinguish between symptoms that are related to one condition versus those arising from another.

Identifying a dual diagnosis involves assessing the interplay between symptoms and understanding how one condition influences the other.

For example, recognizing that substance abuse may be a coping mechanism for depression is crucial in developing a treatment plan that addresses both issues. This comprehensive assessment helps in formulating a treatment strategy that targets the root causes and interrelationships of the disorders.

A dual diagnosis also necessitates a tailored treatment approach that simultaneously addresses both disorders. Mental health professionals must be skilled in managing complex cases where symptoms of one disorder may mask or intensify the other, ensuring that both conditions are treated effectively.

SUPPORT STRATEGIES FOR CO-OCCURRING CONDITIONS

Support strategies for managing co-occurring conditions involve a multi-faceted approach that includes professional care, self-help strategies, and community support. Individuals with co-occurring disorders benefit from a supportive environment that acknowledges the challenges of managing multiple conditions and provides resources for holistic care.

Professional support often includes psychotherapy, such as integrated behavioral therapy, and medical treatment to address both depression and associated conditions. It's important to create a therapeutic alliance that respects the individual's experience and encourages active participation in their treatment plan. This can enhance engagement and adherence to treatment protocols.

Self-help strategies, such as mindfulness practices, stress management techniques, and lifestyle changes, play a significant role in managing co-occurring conditions. Engaging in regular physical activity, maintaining a balanced diet, and developing coping skills can help individuals manage symptoms and improve overall quality of life. Additionally, connecting with support groups and community resources provides a network of understanding and encouragement, aiding in long-term recovery.

CHAPTER FIVE

TREATMENT OPTIONS FOR DEPRESSION

OVERVIEW OF PSYCHOTHERAPIES (CBT, DBT, ETC.)

Cognitive Behavioral Therapy (CBT) and Dialectical Behavior Therapy (DBT) are two widely used psychotherapies for treating depression. CBT focuses on identifying and changing negative thought patterns and behaviors that contribute to depression. The therapy typically involves working with a therapist to recognize distorted thinking, challenge these thoughts, and develop healthier ways of thinking and behaving.

CBT is structured and goal-oriented, often involving homework assignments to practice new skills in real-world situations.

DBT, a variant of CBT, integrates strategies for emotional regulation, distress tolerance, and interpersonal effectiveness. It is especially effective for individuals with severe mood swings and self-destructive behaviors. DBT combines individual therapy with group skills training, emphasizing mindfulness and acceptance to help individuals manage their emotions more effectively. This therapy is structured into four modules: mindfulness, distress tolerance, emotional regulation, and interpersonal effectiveness.

Both therapies require a commitment to regular sessions and active participation in between sessions. They are typically delivered in weekly sessions, each lasting about 45-60 minutes. The skills learned in therapy are designed to be practiced and incorporated into daily life to bring about lasting change and improvement in managing depressive symptoms.

MEDICATION OPTIONS AND HOW THEY WORK

Antidepressants are commonly prescribed for managing depression and can significantly alleviate symptoms. Selective Serotonin Reuptake Inhibitors (SSRIs) are one of the most commonly used classes of antidepressants. They work by increasing levels of serotonin, a neurotransmitter associated with mood regulation, in the brain. SSRIs are generally well-tolerated and are considered a first-line treatment for depression. Common examples include fluoxetine (Prozac) and sertraline (Zoloft).

Other classes of antidepressants include Serotonin-Norepinephrine Reuptake Inhibitors (SNRIs) and Tricyclic Antidepressants (TCAs). SNRIs, such as venlafaxine (Effexor), increase both serotonin and norepinephrine levels, which can help alleviate depressive symptoms. TCAs, like amitriptyline, are older medications that can be effective but are less commonly used due to their side effect profile. Each medication works differently and can have varying side effects, so it's crucial to work with a healthcare provider to find the most effective medication with manageable side effects.

The effectiveness of antidepressants can take several weeks to become apparent, and it's important to follow the prescribed regimen consistently.

Dosages and medications might need adjustments based on individual responses and side effects. Regular follow-ups with a healthcare provider are essential to monitor progress and make any necessary adjustments to the treatment plan.

COMPLEMENTARY AND ALTERNATIVE TREATMENTS

Complementary and alternative treatments can play a supportive role in managing depression, often used alongside traditional therapies. Practices like mindfulness meditation and yoga can help reduce stress and improve mood by promoting relaxation and self-awareness. Mindfulness meditation involves focusing on the present moment and accepting it without judgment, which can help manage the symptoms of depression and enhance overall well-being.

Nutritional supplements, such as omega-3 fatty acids and vitamin D, have shown some promise in improving mood. Omega-3 fatty acids, found in fish oil, are believed to affect neurotransmitter function and reduce inflammation, which may contribute to better mood regulation. Vitamin D, which can be deficient in some individuals, plays a role in brain function and mood stabilization. It's important to consult with a healthcare provider before starting any new supplements to ensure they are safe and appropriate for individual needs.

Herbal remedies, such as St. John's Wort, are sometimes used to alleviate depressive symptoms, but they can interact with other medications and have side effects. It's crucial to discuss these treatments with a healthcare provider to ensure they do not interfere with conventional treatments or exacerbate symptoms.

THE ROLE OF LIFESTYLE CHANGES

Lifestyle changes can significantly impact the management of depression and overall mental health. Regular physical exercise is known to boost mood by increasing the release of endorphins, which are natural mood enhancers.

Exercise also helps reduce stress and improve sleep quality, which can contribute to better mental health. Incorporating activities such as walking, jogging, or swimming into a daily routine can be beneficial.

Dietary changes can also play a role in managing depression. A balanced diet rich in fruits, vegetables, whole grains, and lean proteins can support brain health and overall well-being. Foods high in antioxidants and omega-3 fatty acids can be particularly beneficial. Reducing the intake of processed foods and sugars can help stabilize mood and energy levels.

Additionally, establishing a regular sleep schedule and practicing good sleep hygiene can improve symptoms of depression. Ensuring sufficient and quality sleep helps regulate mood and cognitive function. Simple practices like maintaining a consistent bedtime, creating a relaxing bedtime routine, and avoiding screens before bed can support better sleep patterns.

CREATING A PERSONALIZED TREATMENT PLAN

A personalized treatment plan for depression involves tailoring approaches based on individual needs, preferences, and responses to various treatments. It begins with a comprehensive assessment by a healthcare provider, who will consider factors such as the severity of symptoms, previous treatment experiences, and any co-occurring conditions. This assessment helps in selecting the most appropriate therapies and interventions.

Incorporating both psychotherapies and medications into the plan can provide a balanced approach to treatment. The plan should outline specific goals, such as reducing symptom severity, improving daily functioning, and enhancing overall quality of life. Regular monitoring and adjustments to the plan based on progress and feedback are essential to ensure the treatment remains effective.

Additionally, including complementary treatments and lifestyle changes can enhance the overall effectiveness of the treatment plan. Engaging in healthy lifestyle habits, such as exercise and a balanced diet, alongside traditional therapies, can contribute to more comprehensive and sustainable management of depression. Regular follow-up appointments with a healthcare provider help refine the plan and address any challenges that arise.

CHAPTER SIX

SELF-HELP AND COPING STRATEGIES

DEVELOPING HEALTHY ROUTINES AND HABITS

Establishing a structured daily routine can significantly impact mental well-being, particularly for individuals dealing with depression. Begin by setting a regular wake-up and sleep time to help regulate your body's internal clock. Consistent sleep patterns contribute to overall mental health by ensuring adequate rest and promoting emotional stability.

 Incorporate activities that foster a sense of accomplishment, such as regular exercise, balanced meals, and personal hygiene. Small, manageable changes to your daily routine can build momentum and provide a sense of control.

Incorporate positive habits gradually to avoid overwhelming yourself. Start with one or two manageable changes, like taking a short walk every day or drinking more water, and slowly integrate additional habits as you feel more comfortable. Tracking your progress can be motivating; consider using a journal or app to note your activities and how they impact your mood. Celebrating small victories can reinforce these healthy habits and encourage persistence.

Maintaining flexibility in your routine is crucial for managing the ebb and flow of motivation and energy levels. Adjust your schedule as needed to accommodate changes in your mood or unforeseen challenges. By developing and sticking to these routines, you can create a stable foundation that supports mental health and helps manage the symptoms of depression effectively.

STRESS MANAGEMENT TECHNIQUES

Effective stress management is essential for alleviating symptoms of depression and improving overall well-being. Begin by identifying your stressors through techniques like journaling or mindfulness. Understanding what triggers your stress allows you to develop targeted coping strategies. Techniques such as deep breathing exercises, progressive muscle relaxation, and guided imagery can help manage acute stress by calming your nervous system and reducing physical tension.

Incorporating regular physical activity into your routine can also significantly lower stress levels. Engaging in exercises like walking, jogging, or yoga helps release endorphins, which are natural mood lifters. Aim for at least 30 minutes of moderate exercise most days of the week to reap the full benefits. Exercise can also improve sleep quality and increase energy levels, further supporting stress management.

Creating a balanced lifestyle that includes time for relaxation and hobbies is another key strategy. Ensure you allocate time each week for activities that bring you joy and relaxation, whether it's reading, gardening, or spending time with loved ones. Balancing work and leisure helps prevent burnout and supports overall mental health.

IMPORTANCE OF SOCIAL SUPPORT

Social support plays a critical role in managing depression and fostering emotional well-being. Building and maintaining a network of supportive friends and family can provide a sense of connection and understanding.

Reach out to those you trust and let them know how you're feeling; sharing your experiences can reduce feelings of isolation and provide valuable emotional support.

Engage in social activities and support groups to expand your network. Joining groups with similar interests or participating in community events can help you connect with others who share your experiences. Social support networks provide encouragement, advice, and a sense of belonging, which are vital for coping with depression.

It's important to reciprocate support and offer help to others as well. Providing emotional support to friends or participating in volunteer work can strengthen relationships and foster a sense of purpose. By giving and receiving support, you build a resilient social network that can help buffer the effects of depression.

MINDFULNESS AND RELAXATION PRACTICES

Mindfulness and relaxation practices are effective tools for managing depression and promoting mental clarity. Start by incorporating mindfulness exercises into your daily routine, such as mindfulness meditation or mindful breathing. These practices involve paying attention to the present moment without judgment, which can reduce stress and enhance self-awareness.

Try incorporating relaxation techniques like progressive muscle relaxation or guided imagery to help manage stress and anxiety. Progressive muscle relaxation involves tensing and then slowly releasing each muscle group to alleviate physical tension, while guided imagery uses mental visualization to create a calming mental environment. Both methods can lower stress levels and improve emotional well-being.

Engage in mindfulness practices regularly, such as through apps or online resources that offer guided meditation sessions.

Consistent practice helps cultivate a state of relaxation and promotes a positive outlook. By integrating these techniques into your life, you can enhance your ability to cope with stress and manage symptoms of depression effectively.

BUILDING RESILIENCE AND SELF-CARE

Building resilience and practicing self-care are essential for managing depression and maintaining mental health. Start by setting realistic goals and breaking them into smaller, achievable steps. This approach helps build a sense of accomplishment and fosters resilience by focusing on manageable tasks and celebrating progress.

Self-care involves prioritizing activities that support your well-being and personal growth. This includes getting adequate sleep, eating a balanced diet, and engaging in activities that bring you joy and relaxation. Regular self-care routines reinforce your ability to cope with stress and prevent burnout, contributing to overall emotional stability.

Developing resilience also involves cultivating a positive mindset and learning from setbacks. Embrace challenges as opportunities for growth and practice self-compassion during difficult times. By building resilience and integrating self-care into your daily routine, you strengthen your ability to handle stress and maintain a balanced emotional state.

CHAPTER SEVEN

NAVIGATING PROFESSIONAL HELP
TYPES OF MENTAL HEALTH PROFESSIONALS

Mental health professionals come in various forms, each specializing in different aspects of mental health and therapy. Psychiatrists are medical doctors who can prescribe medication and often focus on the biological and chemical aspects of mental health disorders. Clinical psychologists hold a doctoral degree in psychology and use therapies such as cognitive-behavioral therapy (CBT) to address emotional and behavioral issues.

They are not medical doctors but are skilled in conducting assessments and providing therapy. Licensed clinical social workers (LCSWs) and licensed professional counselors (LPCs) offer therapy and support, focusing on helping individuals cope with life challenges and mental health issues through counseling and therapy techniques.

Psychologists and counselors may employ a variety of therapeutic approaches, including individual therapy, family therapy, and group therapy. They are trained to handle different mental health issues and can provide support in both short-term and long-term settings.

Their training allows them to offer evidence-based treatments tailored to each individual's needs. Additionally, marriage and family therapists (MFTs) specialize in addressing issues within family units and relationships, providing guidance and support to improve communication and resolve conflicts.

Each type of professional plays a unique role in the mental health landscape, and understanding their differences can help individuals choose the best fit for their needs. It's essential to consider what specific type of support is required—whether it's medication management, psychotherapy, or a combination of both—when selecting a mental health professional.

HOW TO FIND THE RIGHT THERAPIST OR COUNSELOR

Finding the right therapist or counselor involves several steps to ensure a good match between your needs and the professional's expertise. Start by researching professionals in your area who specialize in the issues you're facing, such as depression, anxiety, or relationship problems. You can use online directories, ask for referrals from your primary care doctor, or get recommendations from friends and family. Look for professionals with relevant qualifications and experience, and consider reading reviews or testimonials to gauge their effectiveness.

Once you have a list of potential therapists, schedule initial consultations to discuss your needs and their approach to therapy. This is often referred to as a "pre-therapy" or "discovery" session and allows you to ask questions about their treatment methods, availability, and fees. Pay attention to how comfortable you feel during these meetings; a strong therapeutic alliance is crucial for effective therapy.

It's also important to verify if they accept your insurance or if their services fit within your budget.

Choosing a therapist is a personal decision and may require meeting with a few professionals before finding the right one. Trust your instincts and choose someone with whom you feel a strong connection and who demonstrates an understanding of your concerns. Building a productive therapeutic relationship is essential for achieving positive outcomes in therapy.

WHAT TO EXPECT IN THERAPY SESSIONS

During therapy sessions, you can expect a structured environment where the focus is on your thoughts, feelings, and behaviors. Initially, the therapist will work with you to understand your history, current challenges, and goals for therapy. This might involve discussing past experiences, family dynamics, and any specific issues you wish to address. The first few sessions are typically dedicated to establishing rapport and setting up a treatment plan tailored to your needs.

Therapy sessions often involve various techniques and approaches, depending on the therapist's style and the therapeutic modality used. For instance, cognitive-behavioral therapy (CBT) may involve identifying and challenging negative thought patterns, while psychodynamic therapy might explore unconscious processes and past experiences. You will likely be asked to engage in exercises or homework assignments between sessions to practice new skills and reinforce learning.

Throughout the therapy process, expect to engage in open and honest conversations about your thoughts and feelings. Therapy is a collaborative process, so actively participating, providing feedback, and discussing any concerns with your therapist will help ensure that the sessions are productive and aligned with your goals. Regular attendance and active engagement are key to making progress and achieving the desired outcomes.

WORKING WITH YOUR HEALTHCARE PROVIDER

Effective management of mental health often involves collaboration between your therapist and other healthcare providers. Your primary care physician or psychiatrist may play a role in your overall treatment plan, especially if medication is part of your therapy. It's important to communicate openly with all of your healthcare providers about your symptoms, treatment progress, and any side effects you may experience from medications.

Regular updates between your therapist and other providers can help create a cohesive treatment plan. If you are seeing a psychiatrist for medication management, ensure they are informed about your therapy sessions and any changes in your mental health status. This coordination can lead to a more integrated approach, optimizing both medication and therapy outcomes.

Additionally, maintaining open lines of communication with your therapist and other healthcare providers ensures that everyone involved in your care is on the same page. This collaboration helps in addressing any emerging issues promptly and adjusting the treatment plan as needed to better support your mental health journey.

ADVOCACY AND NAVIGATING INSURANCE

Navigating insurance coverage for mental health services can be complex, but understanding your benefits is crucial for managing costs. Start by reviewing your insurance policy to determine what mental health services are covered, including the types of therapy, the number of sessions, and any out-of-pocket expenses. Contact your insurance company to clarify details about coverage, pre-authorization requirements, and provider networks.

When selecting a therapist, ensure they are within your insurance network to maximize your benefits. If the therapist is out-of-network, inquire about reimbursement options and what documentation you may need to submit.

Keep detailed records of all payments, claims, and communications with your insurance provider to resolve any issues that may arise.

Advocating for your mental health needs also involves being proactive about your rights and benefits. If you encounter difficulties with coverage or have disputes with your insurer, seek assistance from advocacy organizations or a mental health professional who can provide guidance. Understanding and navigating the insurance process can help ensure that you receive the necessary support while managing costs effectively.

CHAPTER EIGHT

DEPRESSION AND RELATIONSHIPS

HOW DEPRESSION AFFECTS RELATIONSHIPS WITH FAMILY AND FRIENDS

Depression can significantly strain relationships with family and friends, often creating feelings of isolation and misunderstanding. Individuals experiencing depression may withdraw from social interactions, making it challenging for loved ones to connect and offer support. This withdrawal can lead to confusion and frustration among family and friends, who might feel helpless or unappreciated despite their best efforts to be supportive. The emotional distance created by depression can sometimes be mistaken for disinterest or apathy, further complicating interpersonal dynamics.

Additionally, depression can affect how individuals communicate, leading to misunderstandings or conflicts. Those struggling with depression might struggle with expressing their needs or emotions clearly, which can result in misinterpretations and disagreements. This communication breakdown can erode trust and intimacy, making it harder to maintain close relationships. Loved ones may feel unsure of how to approach or support the person with depression, exacerbating feelings of isolation and alienation.

The impact of depression on relationships can also be seen in the increased burden placed on family and friends. The emotional and practical demands of supporting someone with depression can lead to stress and burnout among caregivers, potentially straining their well-being and other relationships.

COMMUNICATING WITH LOVED ONES ABOUT DEPRESSION

Effectively communicating about depression with loved ones involves honesty and openness. Start by choosing a calm and private moment to share your feelings, ensuring that both you and your loved ones are in a receptive state.

Use clear and straightforward language to describe what you're experiencing, emphasizing how it affects your daily life and interactions. It's helpful to express your needs and expectations from the conversation, whether it's seeking emotional support, practical help, or simply understanding.

It's important to approach the discussion with patience and empathy. Understand that your loved ones may need time to process the information and may have their own emotions or questions about how to help. Be prepared for a range of responses and try to provide reassurance and clarity as needed. Active listening is crucial; make sure to acknowledge their feelings and concerns while reinforcing the importance of mutual support.

Providing resources or information about depression can also aid in the conversation. Sharing articles, books, or links to mental health websites can help loved ones better understand what you're going through and how they can offer support. Encouraging open dialogue and ongoing communication can strengthen relationships and ensure that both you and your loved ones feel connected and informed.

STRATEGIES FOR MAINTAINING HEALTHY RELATIONSHIPS

Maintaining healthy relationships while managing depression requires proactive effort and mutual understanding. One key strategy is to establish and respect boundaries that protect both your mental health and your relationships. This might involve setting limits on social activities or finding a balance between personal time and interaction with others. Communicating these boundaries clearly and respectfully helps prevent misunderstandings and ensures that your needs are met without causing undue strain on your relationships.

Regular, honest communication is essential for sustaining healthy relationships. Keep your loved ones informed about your mental health status and any changes in how you're feeling. This transparency helps build trust and prevents assumptions or misinterpretations. Additionally, actively engage in relationships by participating in activities you enjoy and making an effort to show appreciation for your loved ones' support. Small gestures of gratitude can strengthen connections and counteract the distancing effects of depression.

Seeking professional help, such as therapy or counseling, can also play a critical role in maintaining healthy relationships. Therapy provides tools and strategies for managing depression, improving communication skills, and addressing relationship issues. Involving a therapist or counselor can offer additional support and guidance, helping to navigate the complexities of relationships affected by depression while fostering healthier interactions.

SUPPORT FOR PARTNERS AND CAREGIVERS

Partners and caregivers of individuals with depression face unique challenges and require specific support to manage their well-being while providing care.

Caregivers must recognize the importance of self-care and seek their support networks. Engaging in regular self-care practices, such as exercise, hobbies, and relaxation techniques, helps manage stress and prevent burnout. Caregivers should also consider joining support groups or seeking professional counseling to address their own emotional needs and gain coping strategies.

Effective communication between partners is vital for maintaining a balanced relationship. Partners should openly discuss their feelings, concerns, and expectations while also being receptive to the needs of the person with depression. Setting aside dedicated time for conversations about the relationship and the impact of depression can help prevent misunderstandings and ensure that both partners feel heard and supported.

Education about depression and its effects can also benefit partners and caregivers. Understanding the symptoms, treatment options, and challenges associated with depression can enhance empathy and improve interactions. Accessing educational resources, attending workshops, or speaking with mental health professionals can equip partners and caregivers with the knowledge needed to provide effective support while managing their well-being.

ROLE OF SUPPORT GROUPS AND COMMUNITY RESOURCES

Support groups and community resources play a crucial role in managing depression by providing a sense of belonging and practical assistance. Joining a support group allows individuals to connect with others who share similar experiences, offering emotional support and practical advice. These groups often provide a safe space for sharing personal struggles and learning coping strategies from peers who understand the challenges of living with depression.

Community resources, such as mental health organizations and counseling services, offer valuable support beyond what friends and family can provide. These resources can include access to professional counseling, crisis intervention services, and educational workshops on managing depression. Leveraging these resources can enhance one's ability to cope with depression and improve overall mental health.

Engaging with community resources also helps individuals stay informed about available services and support options. Local mental health organizations often provide directories of resources, including support groups, hotlines, and educational materials. Utilizing these resources can foster a stronger support network and contribute to a more comprehensive approach to managing depression and maintaining mental well-being.

CHAPTER NINE

PREVENTING RELAPSE AND MAINTAINING RECOVERY

RECOGNIZING EARLY WARNING SIGNS OF RELAPSE

Understanding the early warning signs of relapse is crucial for maintaining recovery from depression. Common indicators include a noticeable shift in mood, increased withdrawal from daily activities, and a decline in self-care routines. It's essential to stay attuned to these changes and seek help immediately. For instance, if you notice persistent feelings of sadness or fatigue that don't seem to lift, it might be time to reassess your current coping strategies and seek support from a mental health professional. Regular self-monitoring and journaling can also help track these changes, making it easier to identify patterns and seek timely intervention.

Another key sign is the resurgence of negative thought patterns or behaviors that were prevalent before your recovery.

These might include increased self-criticism or avoidance of social interactions. It's beneficial to recognize these patterns early and address them through therapeutic techniques such as cognitive-behavioral therapy (CBT). Implementing stress-management techniques and maintaining regular appointments with your therapist can help manage these early signs and prevent a full-blown relapse.

Finally, changes in physical health, such as disrupted sleep patterns or changes in appetite, can also signal the need for a review of your recovery strategies. Keeping a detailed log of your physical and emotional health can provide valuable insights into potential early warning signs. Engaging in regular physical activity and maintaining a balanced diet can also help stabilize your mood and overall well-being, further reducing the risk of relapse.

STRATEGIES FOR LONG-TERM MANAGEMENT

Long-term management of depression requires a comprehensive and proactive approach.

One effective strategy is to establish a routine that includes regular therapy sessions and medication management if prescribed. Consistency in these practices helps to maintain stability and manage symptoms effectively. Developing a daily routine that incorporates time for self-care, hobbies, and social interactions can also reinforce your commitment to managing your mental health long-term.

Incorporating healthy lifestyle changes, such as regular exercise, balanced nutrition, and adequate sleep, plays a significant role in long-term management. Exercise, in particular, has been shown to improve mood and reduce symptoms of depression. Engaging in physical activities you enjoy can boost your energy levels and contribute to overall mental well-being. Additionally, maintaining a nutritious diet that supports brain health and ensuring sufficient sleep each night can help stabilize mood and enhance your ability to cope with stress.

Building a network of supportive relationships is another critical component of long-term management. Surrounding yourself with understanding friends, family members, or support groups provides a sense of connection and reduces feelings of isolation. Regular check-ins with these support systems can offer encouragement and practical advice, helping you stay on track with your management plan and navigate any challenges that arise.

THE IMPORTANCE OF ONGOING SUPPORT

Ongoing support is essential for sustaining recovery from depression. This support can come from various sources, including mental health professionals, support groups, and loved ones.

Engaging with a therapist or counselor regularly provides continuous guidance and an opportunity to address any emerging issues or concerns. Therapy sessions offer a safe space to explore your thoughts and feelings, helping you develop coping strategies and stay focused on your recovery goals.

Support groups, both in-person and online, can also be valuable resources. These groups offer a sense of community and shared experience, providing practical advice and emotional support from individuals who understand your struggles. Participating in these groups can help you feel less isolated and more connected to others who are facing similar challenges, reinforcing your commitment to recovery.

Family and friends play a crucial role in your ongoing support network as well. Maintaining open communication with your loved ones and sharing your needs and experiences can strengthen these relationships and foster a supportive environment. Educating those close to you about depression and its impact can also help them better understand and support your journey toward maintaining recovery.

BUILDING A RELAPSE PREVENTION PLAN

Creating a relapse prevention plan involves identifying potential triggers and developing strategies to address them effectively. Start by assessing your triggers, which could include stressful life events, specific environments, or certain people. Once you've identified these triggers, develop a set of actionable strategies to manage them. For example, if stress is a trigger, incorporating stress-relief techniques such as mindfulness or relaxation exercises into your daily routine can be beneficial.

Your prevention plan should also include specific coping strategies and emergency contacts for moments when you feel overwhelmed. Establishing a list of coping mechanisms, such as engaging in hobbies, exercising, or practicing deep breathing, provides you with practical tools to manage challenging situations. Additionally, having a list of trusted individuals you can reach out to during a crisis can offer immediate support and help you stay on track with your recovery goals.

Regularly reviewing and updating your relapse prevention plan is essential for ensuring its effectiveness.

Schedule periodic evaluations of your plan to assess what's working and what needs adjustment. This proactive approach helps you stay prepared for potential challenges and adapt your strategies as needed, increasing your chances of maintaining long-term recovery.

SETTING AND ACHIEVING PERSONAL GOALS

Setting and achieving personal goals plays a significant role in maintaining motivation and progress in recovery. Start by defining clear, achievable goals that align with your values and interests.

These goals could be related to personal growth, career aspirations, or improving relationships. Breaking these goals into smaller, manageable steps can make them feel less overwhelming and more attainable. For instance, if your goal is to improve your social life, start by setting small objectives like attending a weekly social event or reconnecting with an old friend.

Regularly tracking your progress and celebrating milestones is crucial for maintaining motivation. Use tools such as journals or apps to monitor your achievements and reflect on the progress you've made. Recognizing and celebrating even small successes can boost your confidence and reinforce your commitment to your goals. It's also helpful to review and adjust your goals periodically to ensure they remain relevant and realistic.

Incorporating self-compassion and flexibility into your goal-setting process is essential. Understand that setbacks may occur and that achieving your goals is a journey with ups and downs. Embrace these challenges as learning opportunities and adjust your strategies as needed. By maintaining a compassionate and flexible approach, you can continue to work toward your goals while navigating the complexities of recovery.

CHAPTER TEN

DETAILED FAQS

HOW CAN I DIFFERENTIATE BETWEEN DEPRESSION AND A TEMPORARY BAD MOOD?

Depression and a temporary bad mood can be challenging to distinguish, but recognizing the key differences can help. Depression is characterized by persistent feelings of sadness, hopelessness, or emptiness that last for at least two weeks.

Unlike a temporary bad mood, which might arise from a specific event or situation and usually resolves on its own, depression involves a pervasive sense of emotional numbness or distress that affects daily functioning. Individuals with depression often experience a loss of interest in activities they once enjoyed, difficulties in concentration, and changes in sleep or appetite.

Another critical difference is the intensity and duration of the symptoms.

While a temporary bad mood can fluctuate and improve with time, depression presents with more severe and ongoing symptoms. For example, individuals with depression might struggle to get out of bed, maintain relationships, or perform daily tasks, even when there is no clear trigger. This persistent impact on life, coupled with the depth of emotional suffering, distinguishes depression from a fleeting low mood.

It's also important to consider the impact on overall well-being. A temporary bad mood typically doesn't interfere with one's ability to function in various areas of life, whereas depression can significantly impair personal, professional, and social aspects.

If you find that feelings of sadness or hopelessness are lasting longer than a couple of weeks and interfering with your daily life, it may be time to seek professional help to assess whether you're experiencing depression.

WHAT SHOULD I DO IF I EXPERIENCE SUICIDAL THOUGHTS?

If you are experiencing suicidal thoughts, it's crucial to seek immediate support. Reach out to a mental health professional, counselor, or therapist who can provide a safe space to talk about what you're going through. These professionals are trained to offer support and interventions that can help you navigate through these distressing feelings. Additionally, contacting a crisis hotline can provide immediate assistance and connect you with resources to help manage your thoughts and emotions.

It's also essential to confide in trusted friends or family members. Sharing your thoughts with someone who cares about you can provide emotional relief and support. It's important to communicate openly and honestly about how you're feeling so that others can offer help and encourage you to seek professional assistance. Remember, reaching out for help is a sign of strength and the first step towards getting the support you need.

Taking practical steps to ensure your immediate safety is vital. This might involve removing any means of self-harm from your environment, creating a safety plan with a mental health professional, and avoiding situations or places that may exacerbate your feelings. Prioritizing safety, seeking support, and engaging with professional resources are critical actions in managing suicidal thoughts and beginning the journey toward recovery.

HOW CAN I FIND AFFORDABLE MENTAL HEALTH CARE?

Finding affordable mental health care involves exploring various resources and options. Start by researching community mental health centers, which often provide sliding scale fees based on income. These centers offer a range of services, including therapy and counseling, at reduced costs. Many of these facilities receive funding to support individuals who are uninsured or underinsured, making them a viable option for affordable care.

Additionally, consider looking into non-profit organizations and support groups that offer mental health services. Some organizations provide free or low-cost counseling sessions and support groups designed to help individuals manage their mental health. Websites like 211.org can help you locate local resources and services that fit your needs and budget.

Another option is to check if you qualify for government assistance programs such as Medicaid, which offers coverage for mental health services. Many insurance plans also cover mental health care, so reviewing your plan's benefits and speaking with your insurance provider can help you understand what services are covered. Exploring these various options can help you find affordable and accessible mental health care tailored to your financial situation.

ARE THERE ANY LIFESTYLE CHANGES THAT CAN HELP MANAGE DEPRESSION?

Making certain lifestyle changes can significantly aid in managing depression.

Incorporating regular physical exercise into your routine has been shown to improve mood and overall mental health. Activities such as walking, running, or participating in sports can release endorphins and serotonin, which help elevate mood and reduce symptoms of depression. Aim for at least 30 minutes of moderate exercise most days of the week to experience these benefits.

Another important lifestyle change is to establish a consistent sleep schedule. Poor sleep patterns can exacerbate symptoms of depression, so ensuring you get adequate rest each night is crucial. Create a calming bedtime routine, avoid stimulants like caffeine before bed, and maintain a regular sleep schedule to improve the quality of your sleep and support overall mental well-being.

Additionally, adopting a balanced diet and staying hydrated can contribute to better mental health. Nutrient-rich foods such as fruits, vegetables, whole grains, and lean proteins can positively impact your mood and energy levels.

Reducing the intake of processed foods, sugar, and alcohol can also help stabilize your mood and support your mental health. By integrating these lifestyle changes, you can create a supportive environment for managing depression.

WHAT SHOULD I ASK MY DOCTOR WHEN DISCUSSING DEPRESSION TREATMENT OPTIONS?

When discussing depression treatment options with your doctor, it's important to ask about the different types of treatments available. Inquire about both pharmacological options, such as antidepressants, and non-pharmacological therapies, including psychotherapy or counseling. Understanding the benefits and potential side effects of each treatment can help you make informed decisions about your care.

Ask your doctor about the expected timeline for seeing improvements with each treatment option. This will help you set realistic expectations and understand how long it may take before you start feeling better. Additionally, discuss how treatment will be monitored and adjusted based on your progress and any side effects you may experience.

Explore how lifestyle factors and self-care can complement your treatment plan. Ask for recommendations on integrating exercise, nutrition, and other wellness practices into your routine to support your overall mental health. Your doctor can guide how these elements can enhance the effectiveness of your treatment and contribute to your overall well-being.